# Empaths' Book Of Energy Shields—1-Minute Remove Negative Energies & People Now

## Kate Evans

# Introduction

Are you unknowingly attracting negative people and situations into your life which leave you emotionally drained and physically exhausted? To make matters worse you often have difficulties saying "no" to other people's requests - be it last minute babysitting for a friend or letting your ex-college pal crash on your couch indefinitely. To add insult to injury, family and friends have sometimes called and misunderstood you as "sensitive" or a "softie".

Would you like to break free from them once and for all?

In this book you will discover how to block and remove negative energies, people and situations around you tactfully so that they don't keep draining your precious energy and time. You will also be shown a simple 5-minute action plan to help you restore and heal your energy so that you will no longer be on energy deficit.

Whether you have just discovered your empath gifts or are a seasoned empath, you'll benefit from the simple action plan to help you kick-start your energy healing. By the end of this book you will not only know how to identify and stop the energy leaks that are causing you to be energetically exhausted but you will also begin to feel more alive as your energy healing begins.

The best part is you will now finally have the energy to start doing all the things you truly enjoy!

"Sometimes the smallest step in the right direction ends up being the biggest step of your life. Tip Toe if you must, but take the step." - Naeem Callaway

# Table of Contents

**Introduction** — 3

**Chapter 1: How To Tell If You Are An Empath** — 9
*Empaths' Checklist Of Common Traits* — 10

**Chapter 2: Does Energy Healing Work?** — 13
*Types Of Energy Healing* — 13

**Chapter 3: Identifying And Stopping Your Energy Leaks** — 15
*Common Sources Of Energy Leaks* — 16
*Symptoms Of Energy Leaks* — 22
*How To Observe Your Energy Leaks* — 22

**Chapter 4: Simple Action Plan You Can Use In 5-Minute For Energy Healing** — 23

**Conclusion** — 48

**Text Copyright © 2018 Kate Evans**

All rights reserved. No part of this guide may be reproduced in any form without permission in writing from the publisher except in the case of brief quotations embodied in critical articles or reviews.

**Legal & Disclaimer**

The information contained in this book and its contents is not designed to replace nor take the place of any form of medical or professional advice; it is not meant to replace the need for independent medical, financial, legal or other professional advice or services, as may be required. The content and information in this book has been provided for educational and entertainment purposes only.

The content and information contained in this book has been compiled from sources deemed reliable, and it is accurate to the best of the Author's knowledge, information and belief. However, the Author cannot guarantee its accuracy and validity and cannot be held liable for any errors and/or omissions. Further, changes are periodically made to this book as and when needed. Where appropriate and/or necessary, you must consult a professional (including but not limited to your doctor, attorney, financial advisor or such other professional advisor) before using any of the suggested remedies, techniques, or information in this book.

Upon using the contents and information contained in this book, you agree to hold harmless the Author from and against any damages, costs, and expenses, including any legal fees potentially resulting from the application of any of the information provided by this book. This disclaimer applies to any loss, damages or injury caused by the use and application, whether directly or indirectly, of any advice or information presented, whether for breach of contract, tort, negligence, personal injury, criminal intent, or under any other cause of action.

You agree to accept all risks of using the information presented inside this book.

You agree that by continuing to read this book, where appropriate and/or necessary, you shall consult a professional (including but not limited to your doctor, attorney, or financial advisor or such other advisor as needed) before using any of the suggested remedies, techniques, or information in this book. While the book refers to real-life situations, the names mentioned may have been changed.

# Chapter 1: How To Tell If You Are An Empath

If you are reading this book, you probably already know or suspect you are an empath.

You tend to be very insightful and understand how others around you feel. That is why people generally feel good about themselves around you. However, the downside is you might unknowingly take on other people's negative emotions or even their physical pain.

Among your family and friends, you are known as the "good listener" that everyone goes to for their problems or a shoulder to cry on. Even acquaintances and strangers find themselves opening up to you with their personal issues. While you are good for these hurting people and often they walk away feeling much better and lighter, you end up not knowing what to do with their emotional baggage. Sometimes it affects you so much that you feel emotionally drained and physically tired. Such situations are common occurrences for you, unless you learn how to say no or recognize this repeated pattern in your life.

In your personal and work life you tend to avoid any form of conflict like the plague to the exasperation of others. You are usually non-committal to any strong opinions and often bend backwards to keep the peace at home or at work. You are also the peacemaker in most conflicts. However when things get too intense or unbearable for you, you often feel such emotional and physical discomfort that you have sleepless nights. In extreme cases when pushed to your limits, you sometimes do the most unthinkable and uncharacteristic things like ex-communicating from everyone. It is not unusual for an empath when pushed to his or her limits to just walk away from long-term relationships without any warning. The truth is they probably have been enduring the stress for many years before the last straw that broke the camel's back. If you look back over the years, you might recognize some relationships or friendships you have walked away from.

Physically you might be highly sensitive to sensory input like loud noises, sight or smells. You can be easily startled by thunder and lightning. Loud noises or pungent smells can sometimes give you headaches. Even taking too much caffeine like coffees can make you jittery or irritable. Sad movies or books make your heart wrench more than the average person. In general you do not fare well in crowded places like shopping malls as they tend to make you feel drained. The word "retail therapy" is definitely not for empaths who fare best in nature like in parks, forests or the beach to recharge.

In general you are an even-tempered person but can appear as introverted, shy or moody to others as they don't understand that you sometimes need solitude to recharge. Others may sometimes get exasperated with you and label you as overly-sensitive.

Now that you have come to recognize yourself as an empath and embrace your uniqueness, it's time to discover simple but effective methods to support your empathic gift and energy field.

# Empaths' Checklist Of Common Traits

- Warmth, understanding and compassionate

- Gift of knowing about things beyond intuition or gut feeling and can become stronger as they become more attuned

- Tend to be problem solvers or thinkers with the ability to tap into Universal knowledge as they are often receptive to divine guidance

- Tend to daydream and can stare into space for hours if not kept stimulated in work or life, and might have difficulties focusing on the mundane

- Good listeners with an innate ability to feel and perceive other people's energies and emotions as their own, which sometimes make them a dumping ground for others

- Can sense other people's emotions or bad thoughts even from a great distance

- Susceptible to mood swings and can appear moody, aloof or unsociable if they have taken on too much of other people's negative energies, thoughts, wishes and moods

- Highly sensitive to emotions or physical symptoms of others and can sometimes catch sympathy pains like colds or body aches of closest family or friends

- Sensitive to sensory input and find crowded places like shopping malls or stadiums overwhelming

- Tend to avoid TV, news or movies that depict sadness, cruelty or violence in humankind, children or animals as they are deeply affected and unbearable for them

- Prone to ailments like digestive disorders, aches and pains

- Prone to chronic fatigue even after sleeping many hours as their energy drain cannot be cured by sleep alone

- Can become addicted to alcohol, drugs, food or sex as a form of self protection to block out emotions of others or self

- Can become reclusive and unresponsive at times when overwhelmed or struggling with emotional baggage from self or others

- Dislike and will avoid any form of disharmony or conflict

- Tend to bottle up feelings or create barriers till they explode without warning

- Drawn to the metaphysical like paranormal, NDE (Near Death Experience), holistic therapies and anything supernatural e.g. Chakra, Reiki, Fengshui, crystals etc.

- Prefers solitude and spending quiet time in nature or with animals

- Can be misunderstood as lazy if they are forced to be in jobs they dislike

- A seeker of knowledge and truth but might lead to information overload

- Dislike narcissism and overly egotistical people who put themselves before others

- Avoid buying antiques or pre-loved items as they carry the previous owner's energy

- Some avoid meat or become vegetarians as they can sense the vibrations of the animals in meat and poultry

# Chapter 2: Does Energy Healing Work?

Does energy healing really work? Just like you don't need be a physicist to uncerstand the law of gravity for it to work, neither do you need to grasp the concept of energy healing for it to work in your life. In fact you don't even need to be spiritual to benefit from energy healing for energy is based on scientific principles.

To put it simply, everything around us is made of visible and non-visible energy. The universe is made up of energy represented in different shapes and forms. Imagine everything you see around you is vibrating a certain frequency, including yourself and your favorite pet.

An example of non-visible energy is the frequency of music. Do you notice that when you listen to music you like, it can uplift your mood instantly? This is because music vibrates at a high frequency which is why we can even be moved to tears by powerful music. Even the act of dancing and singing can raise our vibrational frequency which might explain why many people enjoy karaoke as a hobby.

Now, our thoughts are also non-visible energy For example, do you notice happy people normally have "good vibes" which just means you probably felt their positive thoughts as vibrational energy. Similarly you can also sense the "negative vibes" of an angry person just by being near them. In events such as a wedding or funeral the "vibes" would feel very different too.

In a nutshell, the more we think about something, the more energy we give to it thus making the vibration denser. In return we create our life based on what we have been thinking or rather our predominant thoughts.

"As you think, so shall you become" - Bruce Lee.

**Types Of Energy Healing**

- Acupuncture using needles to stimulate the flow of chi (energy) to balance the body

- Reiki using the power of intention to direct energy to flow to where it is needed

- Reflexology uses meridians on feet and hands to unblock energy and stimulate healing to the body

- Chakra healing is energy healing that works with the chakra system

- EFT (Emotional Freedom Techniques) works like acupuncture using meridians but without needles

- Crystal healing uses crystals and stones that have healing properties as conduits to direct healing energy to flow into the body and facilitate healing

# Chapter 3: Identifying And Stopping Your Energy Leaks

We all start each day with a certain amount of energy also known as life force but some empaths tend to have less energy than others at e.g. 60%. Even sleeping eight to twelve hours nightly does not help them reach 100%.

If you find yourself constantly depleted and lifeless by the end of the day, it's time to take serious note of what might be draining you energetically without you even realizing it. If you do not stop the energy leaks first, all your energy healing will be depleted soon again leaving you at a deficit.

By the way, do you notice happy people like little children seem to have more energy too? Well, empaths don't need to be constantly happy to thrive but they do need a safe environment whereby they are not constantly drained by negative energies or people tapping into their limited resources.

## Common Sources Of Energy Leaks

1) **Energy Vampires**

Energy vampires don't suck blood or turn into bats. They could be any family member, friend, colleague or even strangers who likes to "feed" on people's energy. They try to demand your constant attention by drawing you into their latest drama or emotional baggage.

As an empath you're like a honey trap to these energy vampires who will often target you with their latest drama in life. You need to recognize energy vampires don't want their problems to be solved; they just want to latch on you as their energy source. Learn to avoid them and create boundaries. Lastly, don't feel guilty about not giving them the time of day otherwise you'll be sacrificing your precious energy to them. So ask yourself, who is draining your life energy?

**Common Traits Of Energy Vampires:**

- Drama queens, whiners, complainers who constantly seek out crisis to feel self-importance

- Notorious guilt trippers with victim complex who prey off your guilt by using self-pitying or emotional blackmail

- Narcissistic one-sided relationship of "me first, you second" by using false charm, deception and manipulation to feed their egos

- Domineering loud-mouthed type who are easily angered and prone to making threats to make you feel intimated

- Usually prone to jealousy of other people's happiness

You might think you're showing love and compassion to those in need, but in actual fact you are not showing love to yourself when you've little energy left to support yourself.

2) **Residual Energy**

Residual energy refers to the remains of lingering energy left by a person or place. For example have you ever walked into a room and felt a sudden heaviness in your spirit? You could be experiencing a residual energy from a previous argument that took place before you entered. Residual energy often lingers at war sites or places of sadness because of the energetic build up due to high human population or traffic.

As highly sensitive individuals, residual energy can impact empaths negatively when you unknowingly let it seep into your energy field influencing your thoughts and moods. For example your mind and body could be in disarray for days after someone shared with you their darkest secret. Your mind will keep replaying and reliving their words and emotions. In turn this lowers your energy, mood and vibration as your aura has been compromised. Remember, as an empath you're often susceptible to energetically picking up other people's energy.

Maryanne is an empath who loves helping others. At mid-life she made a career switch from being an administrator to study nursing as she felt her calling in life was to care and help others around her. But ever since she started working in the emergency ward of the hospital two years ago, her health started declining. At first she contributed her poor health to her odd and long working hours. She even sought out natural therapies such as Ayurvedic healing but the positive effects never lasted for her. Her condition worsened to the state whereby some days she could no longer get out of bed to report for work. Defeated she applied for a leave of absence citing poor health. While recuperating at home, Maryanne started doing lots of online research about her mysterious ailments. Although inconclusive her empath intuition told her it was her workplace that was affecting her negatively energetically. Truth be told, she was often emotionally affected by her patients as many are trauma cases brought into the emergency ward. To test her theory, she requested for a change of ward after returning from her month's rest. Maryanne started working in the maternity ward and each day she delighted in assisting and caring for new mothers and infants. A few months later, she noticed she longer fell ill or suffered from severe exhaustion. Maryanne's case is an example of empaths whose energies are leaked or affected when they spend too much time in residual energy environments whereby death or pain happens constantly.

## 3) **Body Mind Exhaustion Due To Over Tasking**

One of the most common energy leaks for empaths is overextending themselves by overdoing or over-committing. Due to their inability to say no to others empaths tend to over-commit themselves to too many projects such as helping a friend to move house or hosting a big Thanksgiving dinner for the entire family etc.

Ann is single and the oldest of the family. She has a stressful job as an accountant in a fast-paced multinational corporation. Being an empath she finds it difficult to express her needs even when her bosses continue to pile work on her. Oftentimes she has to work late or bring work home. Apart from work stress, Ann has to care for her elderly parents by bringing them to their hospital checkups and physiotherapy. Her other married siblings cited they are too busy with their growing family and careers thus forcing Ann who is single to be responsible for their elderly parents' welfare. As if this is not enough, her siblings would take turns imposing on Ann to babysit their young children when they need timeout to themselves. It seems like everyone from her colleagues to family always have something for Ann to do. Finally nearing mind-body exhaustion Ann quit her job, sold her house and moved to another city quietly without informing anybody. You see, empaths' inability to say no can sometimes lead them to passive aggression or drastic measures when they finally implode.

When your plate is too full there is little time for you to recuperate bodily and mentally. This breakdown leads to an exhausted body-mind which in turn creates "holes" for your energy to leak through continuously. To counter this, consciously create time for yourself to relax.

## 4) Excessive Emotional Reactivity

Vulnerable empaths who are pushed to their limits can either implode or explode. When this happens it can lead to excessive emotional reactivity such as extreme anger or crying at the slightest provocation. An empath who is emotionally unbalanced can experience many mood swings throughout the day. For e.g. they can swing from being sociable to moody for no reason other than hearing a sad love song on radio. Empaths who are unable to control or keep track of their emotions inevitably suffer energy drains caused by all these emotions taking up too much energy. For example you might have said some angry words which left you feeling very regrettable for days. Also do you notice how tired you normally feel after a big crying? The ability to be aware of one's emotional response is normally the first step towards regulating excessive energy drain.

## 5) Lack Of Presence

The ones often caught dreaming in class or at work could be empaths who prefer to deal with their real life problems by being lost in their own fantasy world. Some empaths choose to numb their pain by spending hours in their heads imagining their own fantasy outcome or remembering the "good old times". The problem with this method of coping is not only does it not solve anything, but it disconnects one from the present flow and energy is drained when inhibiting imaginary worlds.

## 6) Ambiguous Relationships And Boundaries

We are not referring to energy vampires who are quite deliberate with what they want from empaths. We are talking about your old college friend or a new colleague who to be fair will not really know what you feel or need from them unless you express yourself clearly.

Tom just lost his job and was forced to take on a new housemate to make rent. Fred the new housemate has just relocated from Canada and was feeling very excited to be living on his own in a new country. As he doesn't have many friends in Seattle, he often sought Tom's company and even invited himself to Tom's game nights with his buddies. Soon Tom's buddies started making fun of Fred as his "new twin" tagalong. Tom, being a typical empath, tried to hint to Fred tactfully instead of telling him directly that he needed time alone with his buddies. Not surprisingly Fred did not get his "hints" and continued to impose himself. Tom on the other hand, already stressed about his finances, now has the added stress of Fred's unwelcome company.

The simplest solution to such situations is clear communication and dialogues. Any relationships that are ambiguous and lack boundaries can be culprits of energy leaks, especially if it is a significant relationship such as your spouse. The next time your partner asks you if you're okay with your mother-in-law coming along on your next family vacation, you need to answer truthfully and create a firm foundation for your relationship so that it does not become a source of energy leaks for you. Remember speak the truth kindly and it will be well received. Similarly if a relationship is not working for you and affecting you negatively, learn to let go and walk away.

## 7) **Addictions**

Due to empaths' sensitive nature, they often suffer more than regular people emotionally and mentally. They also often feel over-whelmed, out-of-control or neglected by others around them. It is thus not surprising some empaths turn to addictions such as alcohol, drugs, food, gambling or sex to numb their pain. Unfortunately the aftermath of all addictions only makes one feel worse after the initial gratification, and the disconnect from one's true feelings only results in severe energy leaks. If you do find yourself in this situation, seek help such as a support group in your area.

## 8) **Past Hurts And Wounds**

Hurts and wounds especially those from our childhood can continue to haunt us in our adulthood. Truth be told, few of us had the picture perfect childhood but it is how we processed what happened to us in the past that affects our present. Sensitive and delicate empath children often suffer more if they have insensitive or Type A (controlling, impatient and inflexible) parents who refuse to acknowledge their sensitive needs. If you know of such children or have one yourself, be extra patient and kind to them.

Owen is the youngest child of the family. He was also known as the "accidental crybaby" that came along when his parents were already in their late forties. Owen was often left to be cared for by his older siblings who unfortunately resented their extra duties and often pushed their responsibilities around. Even at a tender age, Owen being an empath was highly sensitive and in tune to what's happening. Because he sensed and believed he was unloved by his family he often acted out by crying incessantly driving his family to their wit's end. His older brothers who were all highly into sports also did not understand why their little brother preferred singing in the school choir. They teased him mercilessly for being different and often commented he was too thin-skinned and sensitive for a boy. Now Owen is a grownup living on his own and working as a highly sought after hair stylist. Owen is also gay and openly so with all his friends, but he kept it a secret from his family as he did not want any unwanted comments from them. Although successful at work, Owen is often unlucky in love as he often doubts his self-worth and always ends up sabotaging his relationships because of his deep-rooted insecurities of being the unloved son. To date he remains estranged from his family and often uses work as an excuse not to visit during the holidays such as Thanksgiving and Christmas. Although on the outside Owen looks like he is triumphing in life he is actually wilting on the inside yearning for the acceptance he never felt from his family. To handle his pain and anxieties, Owen uses recreational drugs to numb it.

Regardless of what happened in the past, you are the only one who can accept what happened, forgive and move on. Holding on to past hurts and wounds will only hold you back and put you in a perpetual cycle of resentment and toxic blame. When you hold on and become stuck in negative emotions it creates a constant drain on your energy and poisons your life. By not letting go you are unable to receive or recognize good when it happens in your life.

## 9) Gossip And Complaining

One main reason people like to gossip is because it often gives one the rush of feeling superior to the office slut or someone's infidel spouse. Do you fool yourself into thinking that it is just harmless gossip? Whenever we engage in gossip or complaints we are in fact pulling ourselves down into the dense negative energy zone which in turn zaps our energy. The next time you walk past the office gossip party, make a detour and avoid them like the plague. Remember what you put out there is also what you will receive. By not participating in gossip or complaints your energy will not be mingled with dense energy thus leaving you feeling lighter and freer.

**Symptoms Of Energy Leaks**

- Unexplainable anxieties

- Feeling of being overwhelmed

- Mental exhaustion
- Scatterbrain, forgetfulness or confusion

- Inability to focus and easily distracted

- Addictive behavior such as alcohol or binge eating etc.

- Inability to decide, commit or complete tasks

- Lack of desire or motivation to do anything

**How To Observe Your Energy Leaks**

When you go to sleep tonight, do not read or watch TV but just lay down comfortably on your bed and try to relax. Start observing how your body feels before slowly bringing your awareness to your upmost thoughts. Do you notice what comes to your mind? Are you thinking or worrying about someone or something? Or are you obsessing about the day's events that have already passed? Are you holding on to resentment towards someone who abandoned you? You might have to try this exercise for a few nights to find out what are your predominant thoughts. If you often have thoughts or resentment about the past it could be past hurts that are causing your energy to leak. If you constantly worry about your job, it could be the hostile environment that is zapping your energy. Or perhaps you are losing sleep over your sister's latest love drama with a married man (she could be an energy vampire in your life). Observe your thoughts as they arise each night but don't make judgment on them. Instead try to separate yourself from your thoughts and be a mere observer for now till you decide how best to deal with these energy leaks.

# Chapter 4: Simple Action Plan You Can Use In 5-Minute For Energy Healing

Now that you have identified some of your energy leaks it is time to begin some energy healing. Go through the list below and start using the ones that appeal to you most. Go through all or some of them till you find the ones that help you most. Most importantly keep an open mind as you never know which might resonate most with your spirit till you try.

1) **Mini Mindfulness Practice**

There is a humorous Buddhist analogy that our mind is like a playground and our thoughts represented by monkeys swinging from tree to tree with no apparent destination or purpose. To be more exact we have fifty thousand monkeys or rather thoughts each day, of which many are repetitive ones such as "What if I get cancer like my father?" "What if my son has an accident?" Unfortunately many of us are ruled and plagued by such non-serving thoughts. Some of us get carried away and live in the perpetual state between worry and fear. Constant worry and fear eventually start chipping away at our energy. We do a lot by rushing around but end up accomplishing nothing thanks to the monkey mind of keeping us constantly busy. The end result is physical and mental fatigue which results in a constant source of energy leak. So how do we tame the monkeys, relax our mind and heal our energy?

Don't worry we are not going to do a lotus pose one hour meditation, instead let's start with baby steps first. Today you just need to do one of the exercises listed below. Before you begin each exercise, anchor yourself to be fully present for just a second then another and another. Whenever you become aware your thoughts have strayed come back to the present moment till you have enough for the day.

a) **Mindful Sitting**

Find a quiet place and sit for 5 minutes. Next imagine yourself as the snowman inside a shaken snow globe and the falling flakes as your random thoughts while counting backwards 10,9,8,7,6,5,4,3,2,1. The goal here is to let the flakes (thoughts) settle down. Each time a thought pops up, just say "I acknowledge" and return to imagining the flakes (thoughts) settling on the ground. A good mantra to this exercise is "my mind is calm, my body is at ease".

### b) Mindful Breathing Exercise

Just set aside 5 minutes. Find a quiet place and sit or lay down in a relaxed manner. Begin with a deep inhalation through your nose and exhalation through your mouth. Try to maintain each breath cycle for six seconds. Now start to let go of your thoughts about what you need to do later or what happened earlier. As you breathe in and out observe your rising and falling thoughts. To be more present focus on your breath and imagine with an inhalation the life force entering your body and with each exhalation you expel all the worries and fears you are holding on to. Repeat for one minute or until you feel rested. For best results, do this exercise daily and try increasing the duration from one to two or five minutes. Before you know it, you are meditating.

### c) Mindful Awareness & Observation Exercise

This exercise is one of my favorite as it is simple and easy to incorporate into daily life. The goal is to sharpen your awareness and cultivate contentment in yourself and what's happening around you even if it's just a familiar routine or task for you.

Let's start with where you are. For example you are now reading this book; observe where you are and what you are sitting on. Is your seat comfortable? Is there any smell of cooking? Can you hear birds chirping in the background?

One of the more popular exercises is mindful eating; since we eat several times a day it's really easy to incorporate this exercise. Turn off all distractions such as TV or reading newspapers when you sit down to eat. Take some time to smell your food and examine its texture before taking the first bite. Try closing your eyes and savor your food instead of rushing through it. If you're eating with others, try to minimize conversation. Other simple tasks include brushing your teeth, tying shoelaces, opening doors with your less dominant hand or taking a different route to work.

By doing so you are actively activating your subconscious mind instead of "sleepwalking" through your daily routines. Everyday aim to do some of your regular activities mindfully and you would have accomplished mini acts of awareness throughout the day. Eventually you will start to find yourself becoming more alert energetically and coming up with more creative ideas and thoughts because you're allowing new thought patterns to form.

## d) Mindful Listening Exercise

There's a reason why we are given two ears and one mouth instead of one ear and two mouths. Unfortunately most of us tend to talk more than we listen. During conversations we are often eagerly waiting to interrupt with our two cents' worth especially when we get excited. Gossiping becomes a new hobby for others. Sometimes when our colleagues, spouse or children try to tell us something new we shut them down with our rigid opinions and beliefs without giving them a chance.
Today let's train our mind to be non-judgmental by training our ears. Start by listening to some neutral music or a song that you have no pre-association with, for example a song which reminds you of your ex-boyfriend is a no-no. If you find it difficult to pick a neutral song, play some classical or instrumental music instead. Find a quiet place, put on your earphones, close your eyes and listen to the music. During the duration of the music, tell yourself not to form any opinions of like or dislike. Usually we just accept the music for what it is isn't it? Explore without judgment and just listen intently till you're fully immersed. Do this listening exercise as often as you like. The next time your child or partner try to tell you about their day, listen without judgment and comments. You'll be surprised how much more you're picking up when you listen without thoughts of interrupting or judgment.

## 2) **Blue Ocean Therapy**

Have you ever looked at the vast ocean feeling so small and invincible at the same time? Did going for a swim in the ocean make you feel alive and invigorated? Ocean therapy is an actual program that has successfully taken advantage of the ocean's natural healing properties to treat PTSD (post traumatic stress disorder). Part of the program includes teaching people to surf which showed that when they are totally immersed in an activity it produces serotonin found in the flow state in meditation and antidepressants. One reason why ocean therapy works is because of its purging ability to wash away negative energies and emotions - which is why your problems suddenly seem so "small" in context of the vast ocean.

I accidentally discovered ocean therapy a few years ago when I was going through a depression caused by spiraling financial and relationship troubles. Dealing with depression and stress left me little energy to cope day-to-day. One day I was so desperate and almost suicidal that I hauled myself to the beach hoping that some sunshine and vitamin D might lift me out of the pits. From then onwards although my problems did not disappear overnight, I started feeling better and kept going back. I don't do very much at the beach except to walk bare foot on the sand, soak in the sun and occasionally take a dip in the sea. Today I still visit the beach weekly as if my wellbeing depends on it. Whenever I feel out of sorts, I know I'm due for a visit to the beach. The next time you need to take your mind off something visit the beach and let the ocean heal you energetically.

## 3) Energy Healing With Forest

If water is not your thing, head for the nearest forest or nature park for some mother nature healing. In Japan "shinrin-yoku" means forest bathing. There are even certified forest therapy guides in the United States. This can be especially beneficial for empaths who can feel things energetically to recharge energetically by soaking in the forest's therapeutic properties. Some scientifically proven benefits include improved health and immune system, increased energy levels, better sleep and enhanced mood.

To fully benefit from forest bathing, do not attempt a sweaty forest hike. Instead do as little as possible. Take a leisurely walk and try to open up your senses. Try grounding and connecting to the earth by lying on the ground or walk barefoot (or wear barefoot shoes). This will help to center your body and reset your natural electromagnetic field. If you can't find time to visit the nature park just stand beneath a nice tree and inhale deeply to energize your body or lay on a patch of healthy greens.

## 4) Epsom Salt Bath

Epsom salt bath is one of the fastest and most effective ways to clear negative energies and restore your energy. It is the first thing I do when I need a quick fix whether from a recurring bad dream about a certain someone or old memories that won't go away. Not only does an Epsom salt bath clear away negative energies, it also detoxifies your body by drawing out toxins. Its magnesium sulfate does wonders for insomnia and will leave you calm and grounded. As an empath you tend to absorb other people's energy unknowingly and sometimes it can be toxic or negative. As a result you might experience some accumulative side effects such as fatigue, tiredness, sadness, confusion and irritability. To rid yourself of these negative energies fast, try taking an Epsom salt bath regularly as part of your energy cleansing ritual.

How to take an Epsom salt bath (you can buy this from any drugstore or pharmacy):

- Dissolve 1-3 cups of Epsom salt bath preferably in warm water

- Optional to add 1 cup of baking soda for increased detoxification and insomnia

- Optional to add 3-6 drops of essential oils such as sandalwood, pine and frankincense for energy clearing

- Mix everything well and soak for fifteen to thirty minutes

- Once you drain your tub visualize all the unwanted energy been sucked away

Tip: If you do not have a bath tub, just mix everything in a pail and use a cup to pour over your body or soak your feet in Epsom salt.

## 5) Aromatherapy And Essential Oils

Essential oil and aromatherapy have long been used by energy medicine healers to purify auras and cleanse negative energy. It is very useful when it comes to clearing negative energy in physical spaces. For example you had a big quarrel with your partner and you want to clear that unsettling lingering negative energy in your bedroom. As an empath you probably have walked into a room and felt an emotional charge that makes you want to leave immediately. Sometimes these negative energies are accumulated by their previous occupants, for example a meeting room that is dominated by a quarrelsome and abusive boss or a house whereby the owners often have heated arguments.

An ancient and indigenous method to clear negative energy is to use a smudge stick or wand made of sage. After lighting the smudge stick use the smoldering smoke to purify the area or person. If you are clearing negative energy in your home move throughout every room with the smoldering smoke while visualizing the smoke removing all negative energy. I used the smudge stick when I first moved into my new home to clear the energies of the previous occupants.

For something more convenient and pleasant smelling you can opt for essential oils that carry energy clearing properties. They can be used with a diffuser, spray bottle or perfume when you need to clear energy or raise your own vibration.

- Cypress will cleanse your surrounding energies and strengthen your heart energy making you feel grounded and secure. In ancient Egypt it was considered the symbol for life.

- Frankincense is known for its purification properties and often used in meditation and religious ceremonies. Use this to clear negative energies in the environment, body or aura. Its calming properties will help you feel centered when you are stressed.

- Juniper is a powerful detoxifier that negates negativity by purifying the atmosphere. It can uplift your spirit by transforming negative emotions into positive ones. Use this in times when you feel low energy and need a clearing of mind and emotions. You can also use this regularly to neutralize bad habits, beliefs and attitudes that no longer serve you.

- Myrrh is effective for clearing and balancing energies. It can also be used to promote your emotional and spiritual wellbeing.

- Sage will help neutralize any negativity and create a psychic shield against tensions.

- Peppermint is a powerful astringent for clearing tension and negative vibes.

Tip: Say a prayer or send good positive vibes when using essential oils.

## 6) Himalayan Salt Lamp

Himalayan salt lamps are not only a beauty of tranquility to look at but they a so help increase energy levels and promote mental and physical healing. If you are constantly tired emotionally and physically, place a salt lamp in the room where you spend the majority of your time. You should be able to feel some improvement in a week. At home my salt lamp is constantly switched on. Even my cat instinctively recognizes its health benefits and often monopolizes it by curling his body around it while napping. The reason why salt lamps work is because they generate negative ions, much like how you feel refreshed and energized when you are in the high mountains or countryside. The icing on the cake is it also acts as an air purifier, reduces allergies, promotes better sleep and improves your mood.

## 7) Cutting Energetic Cords And Energy Healing With Angels

Energetic cords are invisible cords of attachment that surpass time and space linking you to your ex, a friend or any relationship. Every time we enter into a relationship with someone we form energetic cords with them. It is also created through marriage vows, promises, oaths or intimacy. Sometimes these soul contracts are still valid even though we have broken up with them. Energetic cords can also be negative energetic attachment to addictions or prolonged bereavements such as loss of a loved one or beloved pet which we can't seem to let go.

To cut those energetic cords that no longer serve you, call upon Archangel Michael, a powerful angelic protector with his mighty sword for help. For example, Anderson often dreams of his ex whom he had a lot of unfinished business with thus leaving him emotionally drained and unable to move on.

### How To Cut Energetic Cords:

- Gently close your eyes and take some deep breaths

- Say "Archangel Michael with your mighty sword of light please help me cut a cord with my ex and restore my energy. Remove from my energy field, body, home and everywhere else this person's energy that lingers. Fill me with light and love where the cords are cut." Sometimes you can feel an energetic shift in the room signaling his presence.

- Give thanks and you can repeat this exercise till you feel lighter.

Angels are not just messengers and guardians of God but also energy healers waiting to aid us. Angels are energy because they are literally made of love and light. All angels have the power to heal you energetically in an instant. Whether you need healing in your mind, body or spirit all you have to do is call upon them for your angelic healing. For example you can call upon:

-Archangel Raphael whose name means "healer of God"

-Archangel Uriel who specializes in clearing old emotions and beliefs that no longer serve you

-Archangel Chamuel whose specialty is in clearing dark energy, life purpose and romance

-Archangel Zadkiel to help with forgiveness of self and others and healing of relationships

Remember angels love to help you but will only do so if you invite them. Start asking your angels for your energy healing today.

## 8) Chakra Healing

Chakra means "wheel of spinning energy" in Sanskrit. Imagine your body is made of seven spinning energy wheels that work like invisible rechargeable batteries. Our energy system cannot function or flow freely when one of these seven wheels is blocked due to emotional or physical stress. The seven chakras from bottom to top of your body are:

- Root chakra

- Sacral chakra
- Solar plexus chakra

- Heart chakra

- Throat chakra

- Third eye chakra

- Crown chakra

All your perceptions and senses correspond to a particular chakra. For example when you feel hurt by your partner it is detected in your heart chakra. Nervousness or tension is normally detected in the solar plexus. Sometimes prolonged negative emotions such as grief, blame and resentment can result in closed or blocked chakras causing an energy constriction.

**Symptoms Of Blocked Chakras And How To Heal Them:**

a) **Root Chakra**

It is located at the base of the spine at your tailbone.

It represents feelings rooted in our daily survival essentials such as food, housing, security and money.

When your root chakra is blocked you will often feel stuck and unmotivated, working on an unfulfilling career, ongoing money problems, often on survival mode to get by, poor body image, feeling of inadequacies and feeling of abandonment perhaps by your own family.
How To Heal:

- Connect yourself to earth by walking barefoot on grass or doing gardening

- Visit nature more often

- Include more red foods in your diet e.g. cherries, tomatoes, strawberries and apples

- The color of this chakra is red, visualize it around your root chakra or wear more red

- Use essential oils rosewood, thyme, myrrh, ylang ylang and frankincense

- Wear crystals ruby, garget, bloodstone and agate

b) **Sacral Chakra**

It is located two inches below the belly button.

It represents our sexuality, pleasure and creativity.

When your sacral chakra is blocked you will feel low libido, inability to be emotionally and sexually intimate, distrust in others for loving you as you are, poor self image, frequently in and out of relationships trying to find the "one".

How To Heal:

- Be kinder and gentler with yourself and celebrate the small stuff

- Include more orange food in your diet e.g. oranges and carrots

- The color of this chakra is orange, visualize it around your sacral chakra or wear more orange

- Take long baths and use essential oils rose, sandalwood, jasmine, fennel and cardamom

- Wear crystals carnelian and moonstone

c) **Solar Plexus Chakra**

It is located three inches above the navel.

It represents our confidence and relationship with self, self-esteem and self-worth.

When your solar plexus chakra is blocked you tend to give your power away and make yourself a victim, bend backwards to keep the peace in your relationships, suffer low self-esteem. Physical symptoms include insomnia, stomach pains, anxiety and eating disorders.

How To Heal:

- Get more sun

- Drink chamomile tea and eat more yellow food e.g. corn, bananas and mangoes

- The color of this chakra is yellow, visualize it around your solar plexus chakra or wear more yellow

- Use essential oils lemon, cardamom, cedarwood, rosemary and peppermint

- Wear crystals amber, citrine and tiger's eye

### d) **Heart Chakra**

It is located at the center of the chest.

It represents our ability to love and be loved, compassion and acceptance for self and others.

When your heart chakra is blocked you are unable to give and receive love freely, fear of loneliness, often end up feeling hurt or overly needy in relationships, unable to let go and forgive, faithless and distrust of the world.

How To Heal:

- Be more open hearted, generous and loving

- Follow your heart and dreams and commit regularly to doing things you love

- Include more green foods in your diet e.g. broccoli, green apples, pears and avocados

- The color of this chakra is green, visualize it around your heart chakra or wear more green

- Use essential oils bergamot, rose, jasmine and lavender

- Wear crystals jade and emerald

### e) **Throat Chakra**

It is located at the hollow of the throat.

It represents our self-expression of truth and being heard by others.

When your throat chakra is blocked you -often feel frustrated because you have difficulties expressing yourself without fear of upsetting others and at the expense of pleasing others. You are also prone to sore throat, neck and shoulder pain.

How To Heal:

- Learn to say "no" to others with no explanation needed

- Learn to speak the truth kindly and it will be well received

- Start singing to loosen up, do it in your car or shower

- Include more blue foods in your diet e.g. blueberries, blue corn, purple potatoes

- The color of this chakra is blue, visualize it around your throat chakra or wear more blue

- Use essential oils sage, cypress, basil, hyssop, sandalwood and rosemary

- Wear crystals aquamarine and turquoise

f) **Third Eye Chakra**

It is located in between the eyebrows.

It represents our psychic power, intuition and ability to see the big picture.

When your third eye chakra is blocked you have difficulties in processing your numerous thoughts leading to a loss of intuition and poor judgment, indecisiveness and lack of life purpose. You might also be prone to moodiness, headaches, nightmares and hallucinations.

How To Heal:

- Practice feeling the energetic vibration of people around you and discern if they feel positive or negative

- Trust and follow your intuition more and give yourself a clap every time you get it right

- Listen closely in conversations with others and pick up any underlying message

- The color of this chakra is indigo, visualize it around your third eye chakra or wear more indigo

- Use essential oils thyme, rosemary, pine, helichrysum and clary sage

- Wear crystals sodalite and lapis lazuli

## g) Crown Chakra

It is located at the top of the head.

It represents our spirituality, divine connection and consciousness.

When your crown chakra is blocked you disconnect spiritually and lack life purpose, clinging instead to material possessions, often feel angry at the universe for not helping you. You might be prone to migraines and tension headaches.

How To Heal:

- Read or watch more inspirational materials

- Start with some mindfulness practice or meditation

- Incorporate regular ten to twenty minutes of "quiet time" everyday

- Include more purple foods in your diet e.g. blueberries, grapes and purple sweet potatoes

- The color of this chakra is violet, visualize it around your crown chakra or wear more violet

- Use essential oils neroli, rosewood, jasmine, rose and frankicense

- Wear crystals amethyst and alexandrite

When all your chakras are balanced it allows the natural energy cycles of your body to flow freely. Another method to heal your chakras as a whole is through yoga. Yoga is not just a popular form of exercise but its postures are also an effective way to release all blocked chakras and clear stagnant energy. Use the movement of yoga to help you release unwanted energy.

## 9) Crystals And Stones - Harness Positive Energy & Healing

All crystals and stones carry unique metaphysical properties which can aid in energy healing. As they naturally come from earth, they can help you connect to earth's energy source when placed near your body. Wearing the right crystals will not only give you positive healing energy but help you relax and re-balance as well. You can wear them as a pendant, bracelet or even just discreetly carry one in your pocket. When selecting a crystal, hold it in your hands for awhile and use your empath sense to feel if it's the one for you energetically.

Here are a list of crystals and stones that help in energy healing:

### a) Clear Quartz

Known as the master or universal healer, its powerful healing properties will amplify your energy level, clear energy blockages, purify and link all your chakras to increase harmony and balance. By amplifying your energy and thoughts it also connects you to your higher self and intuition. Wear this crystal close to your skin to amplify your energy and transmutes negativity.

### b) Smoky Quartz

Smoky quartz contains powerful cleansing, detoxifying, balancing and grounding properties. It is also known as the "let go" healing stone because of its grounding power and will help you move on from any old painful memories, emotional baggage and wounds by infusing your body and mind with its natural calming wellness. Wear this stone as a daily cleanser if you need to release negative emotions such as fear, anger, jealousy or grudges. This stone can help you plug your energy leaks by releasing old, blocked or stagnant energy so that you can replace it with new energy. If you are often surrounded by many electronics such as computer, laptop, fax, TV etc., this stone specializes in recognizing and neutralizing electromagnetic radiation.

### c) Rose Quartz

It is said that the most powerful energy is love and nothing emits unconditional love, compassion and beauty to heal the energy of our heart like rose quartz, which is the stone of universal love. If you are holding on to past hurts or tend to be hard on yourself use the rose quartz to help you move on by forgiving and understanding things from another perspective. This feel good stone which represents the heart chakra will heal your heart and help you flush out old toxic energies and emotions trapped inside.

### d) Amethyst

Walk into a crystal shop and you will probably see a giant purple crystal in the corner. The calming and meditative amethyst will increase balance, peace and calmness in your life as well as protect you from negative energies such as energy vampires. Amethyst, which means "not intoxicated" in ancient Greek, will also help you if you are struggling with any addictions. Known as the intuitive eye its super high vibration will connect you to your higher self.

### e) Turquoise

Known as the healer, the vibrant and distinctive turquoise's powerful healing properties will help you realign your energy field while giving you tranquility, calm and well-being. If you suffer from any chronic stress or old emotional wound, wear a turquoise around your heart as a protective and healing spiritual balm. King Tut and Cleopatra of ancient Egypt were known to use this dazzling blue-green gem as protective amulets.

## f) Bloodstone

Used for thousands of years for its healing properties, bloodstone is often used to purify and detoxify by cleansing the body and removing any negative energy. Wearing this stone will remove energy blockages and boost your energy levels, physical endurance and mental clarity, especially if you suffer from mental exhaustion, confusion, irritability or chronic fatigue. You can also wear the bloodstone as a protection amulet against any verbal or physical threats as well as aid in emotional healing. Bloodstone works the lower chakras by realigning energies and is an immune system booster as it purifies the blood, liver, kidneys, bladder, spleen and intestines.

## g) Citrine

Known as the light maker and manifestation stone, citrine is a positive energy-emitting stone that ranges from pale yellow to brownish hue. Linked to the solar plexus chakra, citrine helps to increase energy levels as well as bringing in energy flow to your mind and spirit. If you often feel you are surrounded by darkness or experience self negativities and doubts, wearing this gem daily will bring you more light and positivity by transforming your thoughts and attracting your miracles.

## h) Black Obsidian

Made from rapidly cooled volcanic lava it is also known as royal agate or glassy lava. The black obsidian is a powerful psychic protective stone with the elements of earth, fire and water that will guard you against negative energies and people. It can block physic attack and absorb any negative energy in your environment. You might feel a warning about certain people or negative energies. If you are having relationship problems or suffering from a broken heart use this grounding stone to clear away all disharmony, bad feelings and negative thoughts. It will help you connect with yourself and heal the hurting parts.

As one of my favorite stones I wear it daily to guard against energy vampires and negative situations. I also place an obsidian egg in my bedroom (or you can place it under your pillow) to clear negative energies and decompress from the day. Wearing this stone will also help you relieve any mental stress, past traumas and emotional blockages as well as restore harmony and balance in your life. This intense stone will work very hard to expel all negativity and toxins from your life.

After selecting your stone or crystal, remember to cleanse it of any residual energies left by other people by soaking in a glass of sea salt water overnight or use smudge or incense sticks to smoke cleanse if salt might adversely damage your particular stone. To re-charge your stone or crystal, you can leave it in a glass of cool water for ten to twenty minutes (check it is safe for your particular crystal) or place it for awhile under the moonlight or sunlight.

## 10) Gratitude Journal

Love is considered the most powerful energy and gratitude the best cure to our negative emotions. If you are someone who enjoys writing and can express yourself better through written words, consider starting a gratitude journal. Every night when you settle down to journal, you use what you're thankful for that day to negate all the negative energies. If you do this daily for twenty one days, you will form a new habit and reap its benefits.

Benefits:

- Clear all negative emotions with gratitude thoughts before you sleep

- Journaling will help you create more self awareness and self reflection by organizing your thoughts and putting them in context
- Gain new perspective from your new observations

- It is a safe way for you to express yourself truthfully

- Lower your stress levels and help you deal with stress

- Turn your pain into joy

To begin just pen down one to three things you are grateful for the day or write for five minutes straight till time's up. If you prefer to use a digital gratitude journal you can download one via mobile app. As you grow accustomed to journaling, make it more personal instead of going through the motion. On days you feel a little down, take out your journal and feel a sense of gratitude.

Examples of a gratitude entry could be something as mundane as bumping into your old college buddy to something more in-depth like "I'm thankful I took courage today to say no to my boss when he tried to load me with another project".

Tip: If you feel writing daily makes this just another item on your to-do list to check off, switch to journaling two to three times weekly.

# Conclusion

I've often been called "sensitive" or "softie" by family and friends. Although it bothered me I didn't realize that I'm an empath until my late thirties when suddenly everything clicked as though the light bulb went off.

One of my greatest challenges is saying "no" to others which really took a toll on my health and finances leading to a year-long depression and chronic fatigue. My journey to recovery started with going to the beach aka "blue ocean therapy". The rest as they say is history. But it doesn't mean I stopped going to or doing the things I know will help maintain my day-to-day energy in a positive light. Just like if you have a chronic condition, you don't stop taking your medicine once you feel better.

As an empath you will feel and absorb energy more than others and you probably also have trouble saying "no". Oftentimes you end up taking more than you can handle emotionally and physically. As a result you might even feel a little worn around the edges. This is why you have nothing to lose by these simple energy healing methods so that you can have more energy to focus on what truly matters to you.

To your wellness,

**Kate Evans**

*P.S. I'll be most grateful if you can kindly leave a supportive review on Amazon and share what you liked. It will really help make the next version better. Thank you so much!*

Made in the USA
Middletown, DE
02 January 2019